Great Historic Debates and Speeches™

LINCOLN'S GETTYSBURG ADDRESS

A PRIMARY SOURCE INVESTIGATION

Steven P. Olson

The Rosen Publishing Group, Inc., New York

To Henry, Eric, John, and Annette, who always kept the debate lively

Published in 2005 by The Rosen Publishing Group, Inc.
29 East 21st Street, New York, NY 10010

Copyright © 2005 by The Rosen Publishing Group, Inc.

First Edition

All rights reserved. No part of this book may be reproduced in any form without permission in writing from the publisher, except by a reviewer.

Unless otherwise attributed, all quotes in this book are excerpted from the Bancroft/Bliss version of the Gettysburg Address.

Library of Congress Cataloging-in-Publication Data

Olson, Steven P.
Lincoln's Gettysburg Address / By Steven P. Olson.
   p. cm. — (Great historic debates and speeches)
Includes bibliographical references and index.
ISBN 978-1-4358-3709-6
1. Lincoln, Abraham, 1809–1865. Gettysburg address—Juvenile literature. 2. Lincoln, Abraham, 1809–1865—Juvenile literature. 3. United States—History—Civil War, 1861–1865—Juvenile literature. 4. Gettysburg, Battle of, Gettysburg, Pa., 1863—Juvenile literature. [1. Lincoln, Abraham, 1809–1865. Gettysburg address. 2. Lincoln, Abraham, 1809–1865. 3. United States—History—Civil War, 1861–1865. 4. Gettysburg, Battle of, Gettysburg, Pa., 1863.]
I. Title. II. Series.
E475.55.O47 2005
973.7'092–dc22

2003024891

Manufactured in the United States of America

Cover images: Left: *Lincoln at Gettysburg*, 1938 oil painting by Fletcher C. Ransom. Right: 1863 photograph of dead Confederate soldiers.

CONTENTS

	Introduction	5
Chapter 1	The Unlikely Rise of Abraham Lincoln	6
Chapter 2	The Battle of Gettysburg	16
Chapter 3	The Ceremony	28
Chapter 4	The Meaning of the Gettysburg Address	37
Chapter 5	A Speech That Lives On in History	46
	Primary Source Transcription	53
	Timeline	54
	Glossary	56
	For More Information	57
	For Further Reading	59
	Bibliography	60
	Primary Source Image List	61
	Index	62

Entitled *Lincoln at Gettysburg*, this oil painting depicts President Abraham Lincoln delivering the Gettysburg Address in 1863. It was created by Fletcher C. Ransom in 1938 to mark the seventy-fifth anniversary of Lincoln's most famous speech.

This photograph shows the remains of Confederate soldiers at Gettysburg on July 5, 1863. It was taken by Civil War photographer Timothy O'Sullivan.

INTRODUCTION

It was only 272 words, give or take a few. The speech that President Abraham Lincoln gave—standing on a three-foot platform just south of the town of Gettysburg, Pennsylvania—was so short that the official photographer did not have time to capture the moment on film. Yet the words of the Gettysburg Address painted a new future for the United States and still ring true for Americans today.

Lincoln's most famous speech was delivered as a small part of a cemetery dedication to honor the dead from the Battle of Gettysburg. The organizers of the ceremony were not sure whether Lincoln would be a suitable speaker. To these officials, the president was not a smooth and polished speaker like Edward Everett, the man they chose to give the featured address. It was decided that the president from the Illinois countryside would be asked to say "a few appropriate remarks." After Everett spoke the last line of his two-hour speech, Lincoln rose from his seat and surveyed the massive crowd before him. He then delivered what was later described by his personal secretary as "one of the world's masterpieces in rhetorical art."

Such is the power of language. Lincoln used simple words and clear ideas to communicate his view of the American dream. This is the story of how Abraham Lincoln worked to make that dream come true.

CHAPTER 1

THE UNLIKELY RISE OF ABRAHAM LINCOLN

The least likely and perhaps greatest American president was born on February 12, 1809, in a one-room log cabin on the south fork of Nolin Creek near Hodgenville, Kentucky. The Lincolns had moved west from Virginia in search of better farmlands. However, Thomas Lincoln and his young family struggled in Kentucky. The Lincolns moved on to Indiana, where Abraham's mother, Nancy, died when he was eight years old.

After his mother's death, Abraham's chores around the house increased and kept him home from school. As the only son, Abraham was expected to help his father with the farming. In Indiana, he was sent to a school that opened about a mile (1.6 kilometers) from the family farm, but it closed three months later. By the time he was fifteen, Abraham's formal education was over. He had attended school for just one year.

An Education of Sorts

Somehow, Abraham managed to learn to read. His stepmother, Sarah Bush Lincoln, owned a few books. Although she

Abraham Lincoln was born in this log cabin on a Kentucky farm in 1809. The cabin measures 18 feet by 16 feet and has one window, one door, a small fireplace, and a dirt floor. Today, the cabin stands inside a memorial building managed by the National Park Service. Lincoln's stepmother, Sarah, is shown in the inset photograph, which was taken around 1864.

could not read or write, she sensed that schooling was important and encouraged Abraham to read. Between chores, Abraham read *Pilgrim's Progress* by John Bunyan, Aesop's Fables, or the family Bible. As quoted in *The Hidden Lincoln: From the Letters and Papers of William H. Herndon*, Sarah Bush Lincoln later recalled,

> He [Abraham] must understand everything, even to the smallest thing, minutely and exactly; he would then repeat it over to himself again and again, sometimes in one form and then in another,

and when it was fixed in his mind to suit him he became easy and he never lost that fact or his understanding of it.

As Abraham became more involved in reading and learning, his work around the farm suffered. His father knew that Abraham was not meant to be a farmer. By the time he left home at eighteen, Abraham Lincoln had grown to six feet four inches tall (1.9 meters). He had only one total year of schooling, yet he possessed a burning desire to be something other than a farmer.

THE ART OF MAKING SPEECHES

In the nineteenth century, speech making played a large role in American society and politics. Without television, radio, or nationwide newspapers, politicians used public speaking to communicate their messages. Standing before a crowd and speaking in a clear and articulate voice, a politician became a living figure to his audience, instead of just another name on the ballot. Like other politicians of the day, Lincoln honed his speech-making skills by "stumping" before small groups of people. In Lincoln's day, many new towns in the country did not have a town hall, so speeches were often given at the closest thing in town to a podium—a tree stump.

For those in the audience, a speaker coming to town was both news and entertainment. He brought information from other parts of the country and, like a traveling preacher, a bit of theater.

Lincoln's next few years were spent in search of a career. While learning to survey the Illinois countryside, to pilot riverboats, and to manage a country store, Lincoln discovered an interest in politics and an ability to speak publicly. A very tall man for the time, he drew attention wherever he spoke. To his thoughtful speeches given around Illinois, he often added colorful tales of growing up in the country.

Encouraged by friends and admirers in the town of New Salem, Lincoln ran for the Illinois state legislature in 1832. Although he lost, he ran again in 1834 and won. Lincoln was faced with the challenge of creating laws in the state legislature. He responded by borrowing the books of a friend and began studying the law in earnest. Three years later, Lincoln was a licensed attorney and a two-term member of the state legislature.

Mary Todd Lincoln was an ambitious woman who took pride in her husband's rise in law and politics. Photographed here in 1846 or 1847, she had given birth to four sons. Only Robert, the first one, lived to maturity.

At a friend's party in 1839, Lincoln met a small, bright-eyed twenty-two-year-old woman named Mary Todd. Todd came from a prosperous banking family in Lexington, Kentucky. Although this smart and lively woman had little in common with the country-born Lincoln, Mary Todd saw that he was a man of promise. They married on November 4, 1842. The following August, their first child, Robert Todd Lincoln, was born. The Lincolns had three more sons, Edward, Willie, and Tad.

Daniel Webster *(left)* enjoyed a long congressional career and twice served as secretary of state. His political ally Henry Clay also spent many years in Congress, during which he became Speaker of the House. Clay unsuccessfully ran for president in 1844. (His campaign ribbon is shown at right.) Abraham Lincoln once referred to Clay as his ideal statesman.

The Whig Party

During the 1930s, Lincoln joined the Whig political party. Founded in 1830 under the leadership of Henry Clay and Daniel Webster, the Whigs supported tariffs to protect U.S. industries, the formation of a national bank, and a conservative policy for selling public lands. As the main alternative to the Democratic Party at the time, the Whig Party gained popularity throughout the 1830s. Lincoln supported its policies and candidates as a member of the Illinois legislature.

In 1841, Lincoln returned from the legislature and resumed practicing law in Springfield with Stephen F. Logan, a prominent and capable attorney. In court, Logan was responsible for preparing the case, while Lincoln used simple words, homey stories, and a conversational style to speak to juries. Their legal practice thrived.

Yet politics still called to Lincoln. In part because they both wanted to run for the U.S. Congress, Lincoln and Logan dissolved their partnership in 1844. Although the Democrats had a strong majority in Illinois, the Seventh Congressional District in which Lincoln lived supported the Whigs. Lincoln failed to secure the Whig nomination for the U.S. Congress in 1844. However, his good speeches around the district and hard work for the Whig Party were recognized. In his work as a lawyer, he continued to travel throughout central Illinois and to develop political contacts. Two years later, he won a seat in Congress.

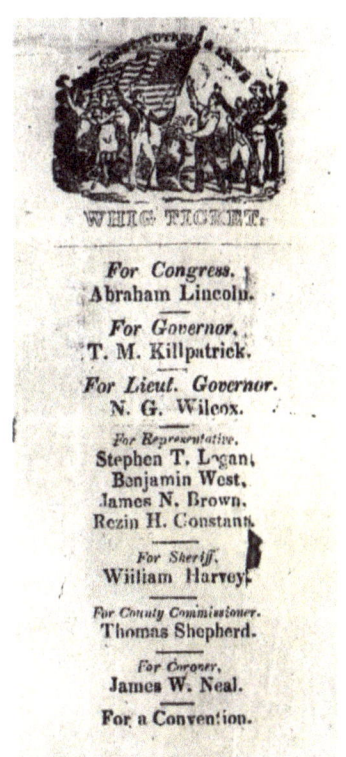

Abraham Lincoln is listed at the top of this handbill presenting the Whig Party lineup for the Seventh Congressional District of Illinois in 1846. The campaign document also includes candidates for state offices.

Lincoln and his family headed to Washington. In national politics for the first time, Congressman Lincoln had to address the issue of slavery. As it divided the nation, so too did it divide the House of Representatives and the Northern and Southern Whig Party members.

Among the many opinions in the Whig Party, Lincoln's voice was a moderate one. Concerning the issue of slavery, Lincoln believed that if

This 1857 map shows the division of the United States between free and slave-holding states and territories. Slave states, all in the South, are denoted in red. The areas shaded dark green were free states, and those in light green were U.S.-owned territories in which slavery was outlawed. These territories later became states.

its expansion was prevented, it would naturally die out in the South. According to David Donald in *Lincoln*, the future president wrote in an 1845 letter,

> I hold it to be a paramount duty of us in the free states, due to the Union of the states, and perhaps to liberty itself . . . to let the slavery of the other states alone; while, on the other hand, I hold it to be equally clear, that we should never knowingly lend ourselves directly or indirectly, to prevent that slavery from dying a natural death.

More than ending slavery, Lincoln believed in the wholeness of the United States, suggesting that he "would consent to the extension of it [slavery] rather than see the Union dissolved." His patience and priorities would later carry him through the Civil War.

In 1848, Congressman Lincoln campaigned in Maryland, Massachusetts, and Illinois on behalf of the Whig candidate for president, General Zachary Taylor. Lincoln urged Taylor to support the Wilmot Proviso, a bill in Congress that would have outlawed the extension of slavery into new territories. However, there was strong opposition to the bill, which eventually failed, and Lincoln focused on campaigning for Taylor.

In part because of Lincoln's efforts, Taylor was elected in 1848, but he died in office in 1850. With the deaths of founders Clay and Webster in 1852, the Whig Party collapsed. That year, its presidential candidate, General Winfield Scott, won only four states in the election. Southern Whigs split off, and many joined the Democratic Party.

After the Kansas-Nebraska Act was passed, pro-slavery and anti-slavery settlers rushed to Kansas. They attempted to influence the outcome of the first election held after the law's passage so that the state would reflect their position on slavery.

Founding of the Republican Party

In 1854, Illinois senator Stephen Douglas, a Democratic rival of Lincoln's, sponsored the Kansas-Nebraska Bill. Its aim was to allow slavery in the Kansas and Nebraska Territory, which was far north of

Abraham Lincoln is shown making his case to an Illinois audience in this illustration depicting one of the Lincoln-Douglas senatorial debates of 1858. Two years later, Lincoln compiled newspaper transcripts of the debates into a book, which he used as a campaign tool in his successful bid for the White House.

the border between the North and South. Considered a compromise by Douglas to Southern Democrats, the Kansas-Nebraska Act was forced through Congress. In the state of Illinois, the new law caused great debate, as southern parts of the state were farther south than some slave states. On May 29, 1856, roughly 270 delegates met in Springfield to organize a new political party to oppose the Kansas-Nebraska Act. The delegates were former members of several different parties. Lincoln played a large role in organizing the delegates of what would become the Illinois Republican Party. He was asked to give the final speech of the convention.

Two years later, the Republican Party had officially formed, and Lincoln, a Republican candidate, faced Douglas in Illinois in a senatorial election. During the campaign, the two candidates engaged in seven debates in which Lincoln stood firm in his conviction that slavery should not be spread and that "a house divided against itself cannot stand." Although Lincoln did well in the final three debates, Douglas was re-elected.

The experience, though, had been good for Lincoln. He was well prepared in 1860, when he ran for president.

CHAPTER 2

THE BATTLE OF GETTYSBURG

A central issue of the 1860 presidential election was slavery, yet political views were not simply for it or against it. One of the justifications for slavery used in the South was the Tenth Amendment to the U.S. Constitution, which states,

> The powers not delegated to the United States by the Constitution, nor prohibited by it to the states, are reserved to the states respectively, or to the people.

How was this amendment to be interpreted? What did the writers of the Constitution intend? Was slavery, which had not yet been outlawed by the U.S. government, to be decided by individual states or the people? Or, did the Declaration of Independence, written eleven years before the Constitution, already free the slaves with its statement that "all men are created equal"? When new states such as California entered the Union, was slavery to be legal, illegal, or decided by the individual state?

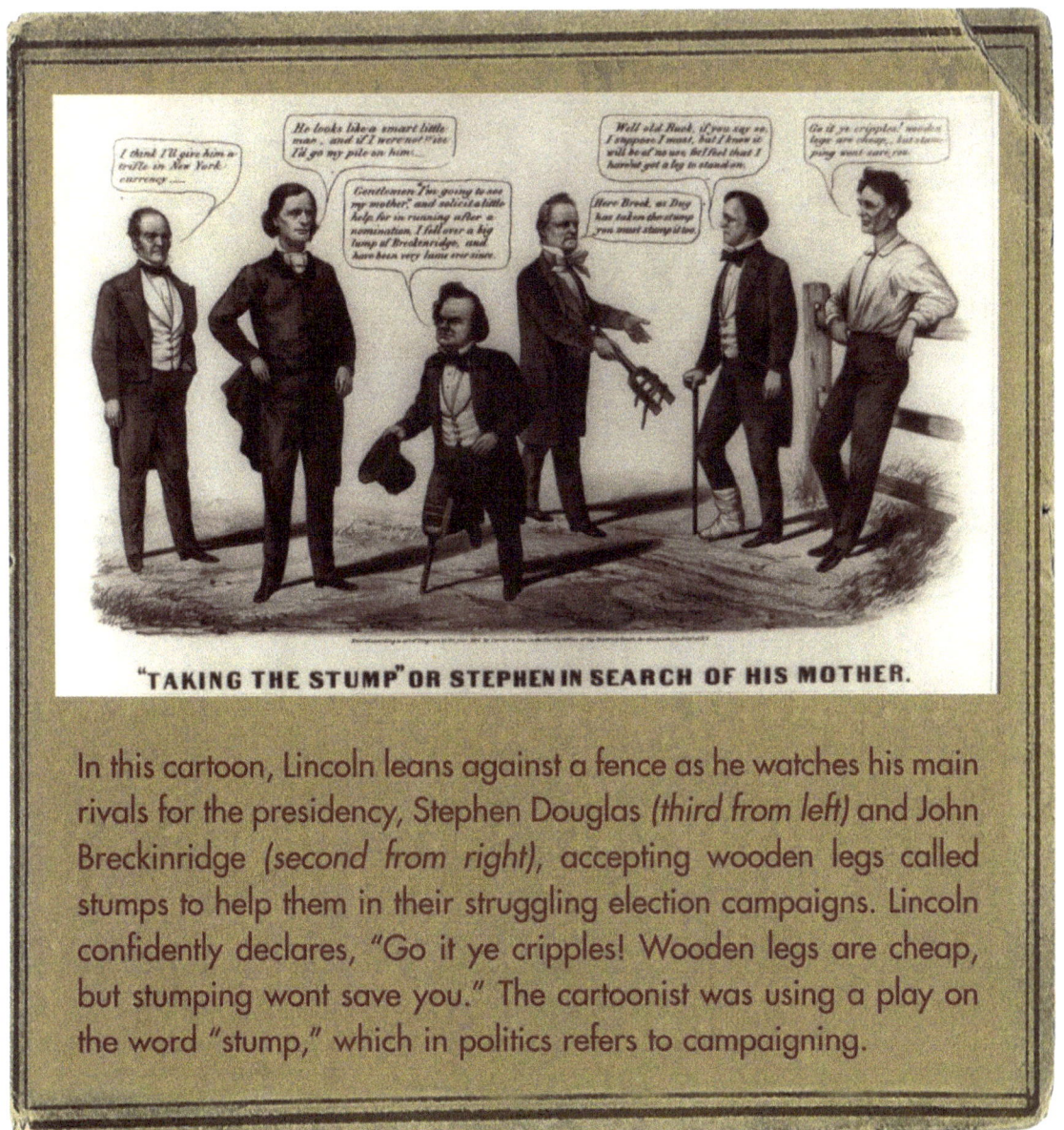

In this cartoon, Lincoln leans against a fence as he watches his main rivals for the presidency, Stephen Douglas *(third from left)* and John Breckinridge *(second from right)*, accepting wooden legs called stumps to help them in their struggling election campaigns. Lincoln confidently declares, "Go it ye cripples! Wooden legs are cheap, but stumping wont save you." The cartoonist was using a play on the word "stump," which in politics refers to campaigning.

Each party had its own answers to these questions, and some of those answers were bitterly opposed by other parties. Even before the election, it was clear that war was a distinct possibility.

The Presidential Election of 1860

Before the presidential election of 1860, Abraham Lincoln was barely known outside of Illinois. During the presidential campaign,

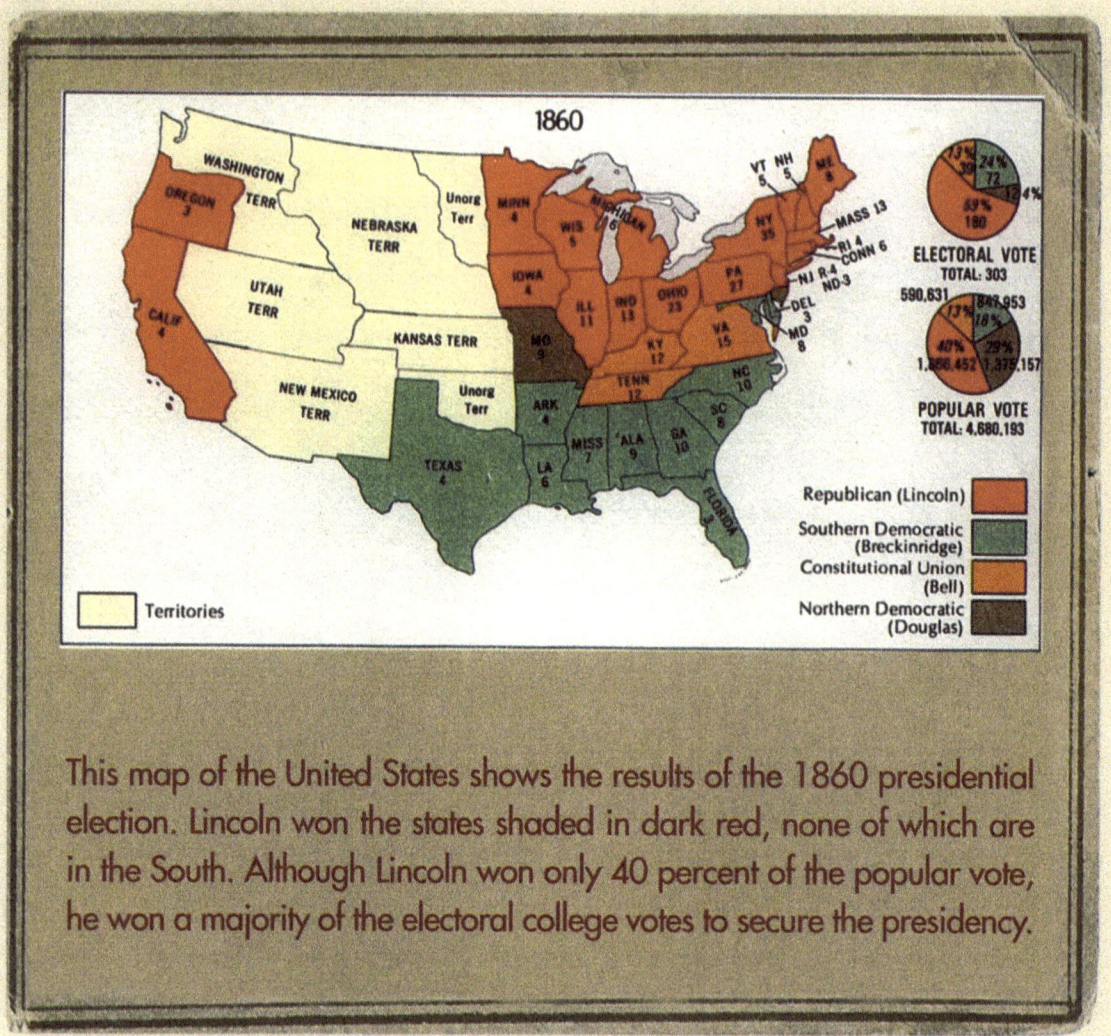

This map of the United States shows the results of the 1860 presidential election. Lincoln won the states shaded in dark red, none of which are in the South. Although Lincoln won only 40 percent of the popular vote, he won a majority of the electoral college votes to secure the presidency.

his supporters carried two rails that Lincoln supposedly split as a young man. The legend of "the Rail Splitter" from out west was born, and a more moderate candidate was presented to the nation. The Northern Democrats nominated Stephen Douglas, while the Southern Democrats nominated the vice president, John C. Breckinridge of Kentucky, who was a defender of slavery. John Bell of Tennessee was nominated by the Constitutional Union Party, which had been formed before the election by conservatives who wanted to preserve the Union and its Constitution.

On November 6, 1860, Abraham Lincoln was elected president by winning every state in which slavery was illegal, except for New Jersey.

He carried no Southern states and earned only 40 percent of the popular vote. The remaining 60 percent was divided among the many other parties and their candidates.

After the election, events began to happen very quickly. Acting on an earlier threat, South Carolina voted to secede from the Union on December 20, 1860. Within two months, Mississippi, Florida, Alabama, Georgia, Louisiana, and Texas followed. On February 8, delegates from Southern states met to adopt a provisional constitution for the Confederate states. At 4:30 AM on April 12, 1861, negotiations for a peaceful surrender of Fort Sumter failed, and Brigadier General P. G. T. Beauregard of the Confederate army gave the order to open fire with fifty cannons. The Civil War had begun.

This hand-colored lithograph depicts the attack on Fort Sumter by Confederate forces on April 12 and 13, 1861. This event marked the start of the Civil War.

1861–1863: A Nation Is Torn Apart

By the end of April, seventeen states, with a combined population of nine million people, had joined the Confederate States of America. While the Union had more soldiers, the first battles outside of Washington, D.C., confirmed that the war would be long and difficult. At places like Shiloh, Bull Run, and Antietam, the Confederate army under the direction of Generals Robert E. Lee, Stonewall Jackson, and James Longstreet showed considerable skill and resistance. Union

At top, Confederate president Jefferson Davis and his cabinet meet on June 1, 1861. From left to right are Stephen Mallory, Judah Benjamin, Leroy Walker, Davis, General Robert E. Lee, John Reagan, Christopher Memminger, Vice President Alexander Stephens, and Robert Toombs. At bottom is a Confederate flag that was captured at the Battle of Gettysburg.

forces failed to manage more than small gains in the South. Tens of thousands of men on both sides died over the next two years.

The Battle of Gettysburg

On June 3, 1863, General Lee's Army of Northern Virginia launched a second invasion of the North. Meanwhile, the 95,000 Union soldiers of the Northern Army of the Potomac were stationed near Washington, D.C., to protect the capital. Instead of attacking the capital, Lee headed for the lush farmlands of southern Pennsylvania, which would provide food for his large army. He knew that if he could resupply his army, he would have a chance to squeeze off Washington from other cities and force Lincoln to begin negotiations for a truce. He also wanted to draw the Union army away from Virginia, since it was in position on the Rappahannock River to make a concentrated effort to take Richmond.

Major General George G. Meade of the Union knew that Confederates were nearby, so he ordered Major General John Buford and 2,500 soldiers to scout to the west. They were followed by a larger body of soldiers under the command of Major General John Reynolds.

On June 30, Buford's party rode through gentle hills into the prosperous farming town of Gettysburg. Stopping at the city cemetery on top of a hill, Buford spied a half dozen Confederate flags at the center of town. A Confederate soldier took a shot at Buford's Union forces, and then the Confederates pulled back out of Gettysburg.

On July 1, the Confederate army returned and attacked, and more Union forces arrived to join the fight. It was combat at close quarters. Soldiers were fighting with their bayonets, fists, and the butts of their rifles. In the afternoon, a fresh surge of Confederate soldiers was able to drive the Union forces back through Gettysburg and up to Cemetery Hill. By the end of the first day, 9,000 Union soldiers had been killed or wounded.

This drawing by Alfred R. Waud presents a view of Cemetery Hill before it was charged by Confederate major general George Pickett's forces. Waud accompanied the troops to the front lines and made detailed sketches of battlefield events.

Fighting intensified the following afternoon farther south along the ridge of Cemetery Hill. General James Longstreet led an attack against the left flank of the Union forces in a rocky valley, while another attack was launched against the right at Culp's Hill. All day long and into the night, the Confederates tried to climb the left flank and Culp's Hill on the right without success. Bodies piled on top of each other until both armies stopped for the day due to exhaustion.

That evening, General Meade received word that Union casualties had exceeded 20,000. Meade predicted that Lee would strike in the morning at the center and moved more men to protect the cemetery

General Meade was widely criticized for allowing Confederate forces to retreat at the end of the Battle of Gettysburg. However, President Lincoln refused his offer of resignation. Congress thanked him for his leadership during the battle in a resolution on January 28, 1864.

ridge. Lee decided that Major General George Pickett's forces would lead a final charge against the center of the line. Fifteen thousand of Pickett's men and 130 cannons were brought into a line just southwest of the town.

Just after noon, the Confederate cannons opened up again, driving Union troops deeper into their trenches. Pickett waited for General Longstreet to order the attack and then could wait no longer. Pickett's men charged up the cemetery ridge just as the last of the Confederate cannonballs was dispensed. Out in the open, Pickett's charge was cut down by Union rifles and cannons. By nightfall, the Confederates were in full retreat, and the patter of rain and the moans of men dying on the grassy hills were the final sounds of the Battle of Gettysburg.

A Most Terrible Battle

It is estimated that more than 50,000 men were killed, wounded, missing, or captured during the Battle of Gettysburg. The South had lost one-third of its men and would never be able to threaten the North again.

This photograph shows the remains of a group of Confederate soldiers lying on a battleground at Gettysburg, Pennsylvania, in July 1863. It was taken by Timothy H. O'Sullivan, one of a number of artists and photographers who accompanied the troops to compile a visual record of the Civil War.

The morning of July 4, 1863, revealed a horrific scene. The 8,000 dead soldiers and 5,000 dead horses far outnumbered the citizens of Gettysburg. On Cemetery Hill, arms of Union soldiers lay across legs of fallen Confederates. Burial parties of Union soldiers, local citizens, and aid organizations moved quickly to bury the dead before disease spread. Graves were dug no more than 3 feet (0.9 m) deep. The stench of bodies hung in the summer heat over the town.

Gettysburg was the first battle in which large numbers of Union soldiers had been killed in Northern territory. Traditionally, burial of wartime dead was left to state and local authorities. However, no one could have predicted that 13,000 bodies would be scattered across this village. On July 24, David Wills, a local businessman and lawyer, wrote to the governor of Pennsylvania about the awful conditions. According to Gary Wills (no relation) in *Lincoln at Gettysburg*, David Wills noted,

David Wills was born near Gettysburg on February 3, 1831. He was one of the town's most prominent citizens in 1863. He later became mayor and was a member of the Gettysburg Borough Council and the director of the Gettysburg National Bank.

> In many instances arms and legs and sometimes heads protrude and my attention has been directed to several places where the hogs were actually rooting out the bodies and devouring.

Pennsylvania governor Andrew Curtin authorized Wills to purchase land for a proper cemetery. He also requested assistance from the seventeen states that had lost soldiers at Gettysburg.

Wills formed the National Soldiers' Cemetery Corporation, which was governed by a board composed of one appointee from each state that had lost soldiers. For $2,475.87, Wills bought 17 acres (6.9 hectares). According to Barbara Silberdick Feinberg in *Abraham Lincoln's Gettysburg Address*, Wills described it in an August 17 letter to Curtin:

> The grounds embrace about seventeen acres on Cemetery Hill, fronting the Baltimore turnpike, and extending to the Taneytown road . . . It is the spot which should be specifically consecrated to this sacred purpose. It was here that such immense quantities of our artillery were massed, and during Thursday and Friday of the battle, from this most important position [on] the field, dealt out death and destruction to the rebel army in every direction of their advance.

The Board of Governors decided to hire William Saunders. He was the superintendent of grounds in the Department of Agriculture and a leading architect in the popular "rural cemetery" movement. With city populations increasing, moving city cemeteries to the country freed precious space and placed the dead in a more natural and peaceful environment. Saunders presented his design to the president and, according to Gary Wills in *Lincoln at Gettysburg*, he recalled in a later journal,

> He [Lincoln] was much pleased with the method of the graves, said it differed from the ordinary cemetery, and, after I had explained the reasons, said it was an advisable and benefitting arrangement.

In his plan, Saunders arranged the graves in a half-circle around a central monument to be built later. Honored with individual tombstones,

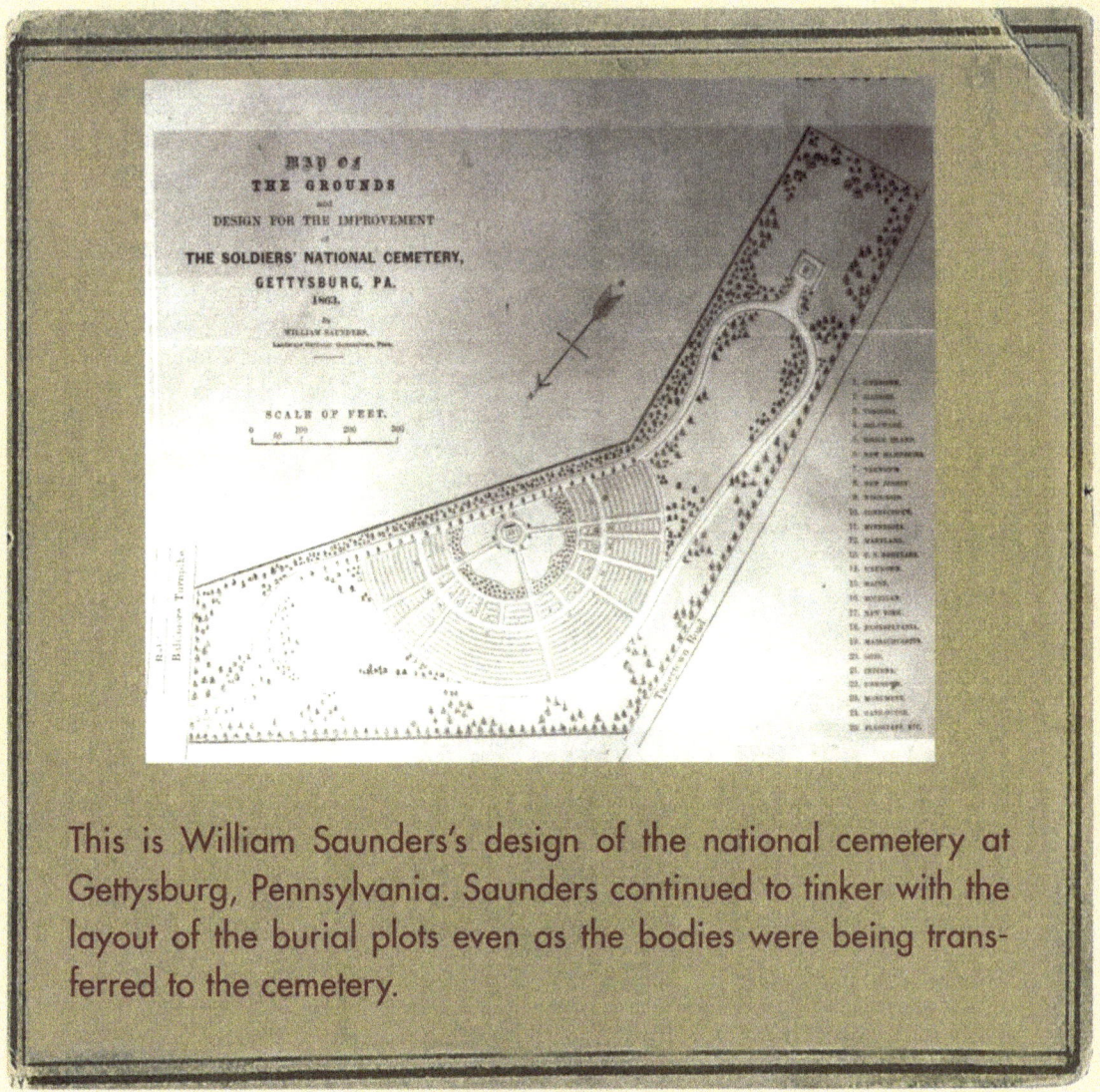

This is William Saunders's design of the national cemetery at Gettysburg, Pennsylvania. Saunders continued to tinker with the layout of the burial plots even as the bodies were being transferred to the cemetery.

the dead of each state were grouped together, with a 4-foot (1.2 m) walkway between sections, and headed by a large, uniform tombstone. No state was given preference over another, and no area was marked for Confederate dead, many of whom were later buried in the South.

As the Union soldiers were taken from their shallow graves and moved to the new cemetery site, Wills started to make arrangements for a proper ceremony to dedicate the grounds of what would become known as the bloodiest battle in the Civil War.

CHAPTER 3

THE CEREMONY

As Wills and the board planned the ceremony, they were unsure of whether to invite President Lincoln to be among the speakers. Although they intended the ceremony to be a solemn occasion shared in the nation's memory, they could have never foreseen that the words of their second-choice speaker would live on in history.

Invitation to President Lincoln

Before the cemetery was dug, Wills felt that the land should be dedicated with a procession to the grounds, gun salutes, music, and speeches. Everyone knew that the foremost American speaker of the time was Edward Everett. A former U.S. senator, governor of Massachusetts, secretary of state, and minister (ambassador) to Britain, Everett had had a distinguished career in public service. He accepted Wills's invitation.

A printed circular was distributed to important leaders around the North. While it is not known if President Lincoln received one, he did send a note indicating that he would attend. The Board of Governors faced a problem: should

The dedication of the Soldiers National Cemetery at Gettysburg was postponed from October 23 to November 19, 1863, because the main speaker, Edward Everett *(left)*, required more time to prepare an appropriate speech. Before entering politics, Everett was an ordained pastor of the Brattle Street Unitarian Church in Boston, Massachusetts, and a professor of Greek literature at Harvard University.

Lincoln be invited to speak, too? According to Feinberg in *Abraham Lincoln's Gettysburg Address*, Clark Carr, Illinois's representative to the board, said, "The question was raised as to his ability to speak upon such a grave and solemn occasion." Although he was a capable speaker, Lincoln's humor came from the rural Midwest, and there was some concern that his speech would be too informal. However, on November 2, Wills sent a letter to Lincoln asking him to stay at Wills's home in Gettysburg and to make a "few appropriate remarks" at the ceremony:

> We hope you will be able to be present to perform this last solemn act to the Soldiers dead on this Battle Field.

The large audience and the gathered dignitaries presented an opportunity for the president to rally support for continuing this long and costly war. In waging war, Lincoln's first goal was keeping the Union together, and he wanted to use the opportunity to remind the country of that goal.

At left, a photograph of President Abraham Lincoln *(center)* with his two personal secretaries, John G. Nicolay *(left)* and John Hay. At right, David Wills's letter to President Lincoln, inviting him to stay at Wills's home during Lincoln's visit to Gettysburg.

Preparation of the Speech

There is considerable debate over when Lincoln wrote the speech that would become the Gettysburg Address. Some scholars have suggested that he dashed off the speech while on the train to Gettysburg or that evening in his room at Wills's house. However, John Nicolay, one of his personal secretaries, noted in his diary that Lincoln used "great deliberation in arranging his thoughts and moulding his phrases, mentally, waiting to reduce them to writing 'til they had taken satisfactory form."

The Ceremony

It is more likely that Lincoln worked on the speech in the weeks leading up to the ceremony. In the midst of his busy schedule, Lincoln may have retreated to his second-floor office in the White House to think about his speech. In the "business wing," as he called it, Lincoln liked to sit at the long table before the windows that overlooked the Potomac. As he regarded the river, 80 miles (129 km) behind which lay the bodies of 8,000 American men, Lincoln may have contemplated how to phrase his "few appropriate remarks." As the featured speaker, Everett was expected to deliver a lengthy discussion of what had happened at the battle, setting the scene in exact detail. Although Lincoln had good knowledge of the events at Gettysburg from the War Department, he knew that the short remarks required of him as president needed to examine the largest issue on the minds of his audience: why were they still fighting this war?

To preserve the Union was Lincoln's first goal, so he could not cast blame on the South. His speech had to find a more timeless tone. A reader of the classics, Lincoln had a strong sense for the rhythmic language of great writing. With the opportunity to speak at such an important occasion, it is likely that Lincoln worked carefully on his speech over a period of weeks.

On November 15, Lincoln confided to Noah Brooks, a journalist with whom he was friendly, that the Gettysburg speech had been written "but not finished." At noon on November 18, Lincoln boarded a special four-car train for the trip to Gettysburg. John Nicolay reported in his memoir that Lincoln had written the first nineteen lines on Executive Mansion paper without corrections to the page; it is likely that earlier drafts of the speech had existed.

Decked in red, white, and blue bunting and American flags, the train stopped at many stations to collect officials and dignitaries. As the train approached Gettysburg, Lincoln excused himself and retreated to the drawing room in the back of the last car to continue work on his speech.

This photograph shows the arrival of the presidential train at Hanover Junction in Hanover, Pennsylvania, on November 18, 1863. Hanover is about ten miles east of Gettysburg. The man at center in the top hat is believed to be President Lincoln.

Dedication of the Grounds

In the late afternoon, the William Mason locomotive pulled into the station on Carlisle Street in a very crowded town. For days, people had been pouring into Gettysburg by train, by buggy, or on foot. Crude seats had been placed into the boxcars of freight trains. Piled at the station were the wooden coffins provided by the federal government. There was going to be a large crowd for this somber occasion.

A layer of low clouds hung over the town of Gettysburg on the morning of November 19, suggesting rain. Before the procession assembled for the short march to the cemetery, the sky had begun to

The Ceremony

clear. At 10 AM, President Lincoln stepped onto Carlisle Street wearing a black suit, white gloves, and a black silk top hat with a band around it. The band was a sign of mourning for his son Willie, who had died of a fever the year before. When Lincoln mounted the chestnut horse large enough for his tall frame, he towered above the procession and onlookers.

The procession left from the town square at 11 AM. Four military bands were scattered throughout the parade and played funeral music. With so much effort placed on burying the dead, the people of Gettysburg had yet to repair their fences or to clear their lands of toppled trees.

At the cemetery, the crowd had swelled in advance of the arriving dignitaries. Only one-third of the bodies had been buried, and open graves drew curious onlookers. On the 3-foot (0.9 m) platform, President Lincoln settled between Secretary of State William Seward and the seat reserved for Edward Everett, who arrived one hour late.

After the opening prayer, Everett rose, bowed to the president, and began:

> Standing beneath this serene sky, overlooking these broad fields now reposing from the labors of the waning year, the mighty Alleghenies dimly towering before us, the graves of our brethren beneath our feet, it is with hesitation that I raise my poor voice to break the eloquent silence of God and Nature.

A skilled orator, Everett was famous for his beautiful voice and colorful expression. Everett had completely memorized his 13,000-word speech. He described local sites in detail. He knew the names of the officers involved. At times, his speech became poetic, recalling the rites of the Greeks to honor their dead. He spoke for two hours, which was not unusual for the time.

THE FIVE VERSIONS OF THE GETTYSBURG ADDRESS

It is likely that the words Lincoln said at Gettysburg do not match any of these five versions in his handwriting that exist today.

The Nicolay First Draft. The oldest surviving draft of the Gettysburg Address, this version was given by Lincoln to his personal assistant John Nicolay. Nicolay claimed that Lincoln held this draft in his hand at Gettysburg. The draft lacks corrections, which suggests earlier versions were written.

The Wills Draft. The organizer of the ceremony, David Wills, asked President Lincoln for the original version of his speech for the official records of the event. It is believed that Wills sent this document to Edward Everett for publication, and it was not returned.

The Hay Draft. To John Hay, his other personal secretary, Lincoln also gave a copy. This version stayed with the family of John Hay until 1906 and was believed to be copied out by Lincoln as a personal favor to Hay.

The Everett Copy. This version was requested of Lincoln by Edward Everett. Although Everett already had the Wills Draft, he requested this version for a book for auction.

The Bancroft/Bliss Version. Written by Lincoln on special paper to be reproduced by historian George Bancroft, this version of the document is the last one written by the president. It is used as the text of the speech for this book.

This photograph shows the crowd around the platform at the dedication of the Soldiers National Cemetery at Gettysburg, Pennsylvania. An enlarged detail of the photograph shows President Lincoln on the platform. It is the only known picture of Lincoln at the ceremony.

Lincoln's Gettysburg Address

When Everett returned to his seat under a rain of applause, Ward Lamon, Lincoln's personal bodyguard, rose to introduce the president. Lincoln rose. According to Feinberg in *Abraham Lincoln's Gettysburg Address*, E. W. Andrews, a reverend, noted from the crowd,

> President Lincoln was so put together physically that, to him, gracefulness of movement was an impossibility. But his awkwardness was lost sight of in the interest which the expression of his face and what he said awakened.

Unlike Everett's sweet voice, Lincoln spoke in an almost squeaky manner that still contained a bit of a Kentucky accent. At the podium, he removed from his pocket his glasses and the two sheets of paper containing his speech. Directly in front of him stood an honor guard of Union soldiers, some with gruesome wounds. He had to have something suitable to say to them.

Before the photographer was able to set up his camera to capture the moment, Lincoln's speech was over. According to John Nicolay, he stopped five times for applause yet concluded in less than four minutes. A funeral song played as the crowd thought about what had been said. The Reverend H. L. Baugher gave the benediction to conclude the event. The crowd exited peaceably.

After attending a meeting at the local Presbyterian church, Lincoln boarded his train that evening and returned to Washington. Exhausted from a long day, the president, suffering from a headache, sprawled across a bench in the last car.

CHAPTER 4

THE MEANING OF THE GETTYSBURG ADDRESS

The following morning in Washington, Lincoln woke up ill and was diagnosed by his doctor to have varioloid, a less dangerous form of smallpox. Confined to the White House for the next three weeks, Lincoln managed the business of the presidency as best he could.

Reactions

Most newspaper accounts of the ceremony focused on Everett's lengthy speech. Even among witnesses of the event, there was disagreement on Lincoln's effect on the crowd. Reliable sources heaped praise on the president for his fine remarks. According to the *Chicago Tribune*, "The dedicatory remarks by President Lincoln will live among the annals of man." To the *Springfield (Mass.) Republican*, Lincoln's speech was "deep in feeling, compact in thought and expression, and tasteful and elegant in every word and comma." George William Curtis of *Harper's Weekly* noted, "The few words from the President were from the heart to the heart." Edward Everett sent a note to Lincoln the following day.

Taken around 1913, this photograph shows the Soldiers National Cemetery at Gettysburg. In the background is the Soldiers' National Monument. It is located where Lincoln stood to deliver the Gettysburg Address. Today, the cemetery is part of Gettysburg National Military Park, which contains over 1,400 monuments, markers, and memorials.

I should be glad if I could flatter myself that I came as near to the central idea of the occasion in two hours as you did in two minutes.

Yet many responded to the address as a political tool of Lincoln's troubled presidency. The *Richmond (Va.) Examiner*, a major newspaper in the capital of the South, called the event a "stage play" with a "vein of comedy." In the *Chicago Times*, a newspaper with connections to the Democratic Party, Lincoln's speech was ridiculed: "The cheek of every American must tingle with shame as he reads the silly, flat, and dish-watery utterances of the man . . . " These writers examined the speech as an instrument of a Republican president struggling to secure another term, not as the president's dream of a brighter future far from the bloody fields of war.

What Lincoln Meant

What did Lincoln intend to communicate with these 272 words spoken on a clear morning in Pennsylvania? In his speech, he did not even mention Pennsylvania. Nor did he mention the town of Gettysburg. He mentioned neither a North nor a South and assigned no blame for the battle. In failing to name any events, dates, or places, Lincoln gave his speech a timeless quality. As much as his address was directed to the 20,000 people gathered at Gettysburg, it was also addressed to Americans of the future.

What then was Lincoln attempting to communicate to the people in front of him? To the political leaders on the stage with him? To the nation as a whole? And to the people who might be reading it 140 years later?

The Gettysburg Address begins,

> Four score and seven years ago our fathers brought forth on this continent, a new nation, conceived in Liberty, and dedicated to the proposition that all men are created equal.

Speaking in 1863, Lincoln began by drawing the attention of his listeners to a significant occasion of the past. The word "score" is an old-fashioned way of referring to twenty. Therefore, "four score" means eighty. Eighty-seven years before 1863 was 1776, the year when the Declaration of Independence was signed. Lincoln was suggesting that the nation was born with the signing of the Declaration of Independence.

Why is this significant? One of the main arguments behind the Confederacy's secession from the Union was in the Tenth Amendment. The Tenth Amendment was part of the Bill of Rights in the United States Constitution, which was signed eleven years after the Declaration of Independence. By mentioning this earlier document, Lincoln was asking his audience to look at the Declaration of Independence, instead of the Constitution, for the meaning of the United States.

In 1776, Lincoln said, our fathers founded a nation in which "all men are created equal." Since the writing of the Declaration of Independence, the meaning of that phrase had been debated and fought over. After all, many of the signers of the declaration, including Lincoln's hero Thomas Jefferson, owned slaves, yet the slaves were not freed with the signing of the document. Although Lincoln had freed slaves in the Confederacy with the Emancipation Proclamation earlier in the year, they had not yet become free people. In the North, Lincoln received constant pressure to emphasize that the reason for fighting the war was to keep the Union together and not to free the slaves. Indeed, Lincoln himself would have agreed that the first goal above all others was to keep the Union together. Why then would the president place this statement in his speech, angering many potential supporters?

In an 1859 letter to Henry L. Pierce, Lincoln honored Thomas Jefferson, the writer of the Declaration of Independence:

> All honor to Jefferson—to the man who, in the concrete pressure of a struggle for national independence by a single person, had the coolness, forecast, and capacity to introduce into a merely revolutionary document, an abstract truth, applicable to all men

This painting by Jean Leon Gerome Ferris depicts Thomas Jefferson *(standing)* working on the Declaration of Independence with Benjamin Franklin *(left)* and John Adams in Jefferson's home in Philadelphia. Abraham Lincoln drew inspiration from Thomas Jefferson and the Declaration of Independence while he was drafting the Gettysburg Address.

> and all times, and so to embalm it there, that today, and in all coming days, it shall be a rebuke and a stumbling-block to the very harbingers of reappearing tyranny and oppression.

In adding the phrase "all men are created equal" to the Gettysburg Address, Lincoln had placed a similar "abstract truth." In referring to Jefferson's phrase, Lincoln was suggesting that imperfect as America may have been, Americans could always look to improve the nation to approach the ideal of equality for all men, as defined at America's birth.

> Now we are engaged in a great civil war, testing whether that nation, or any nation so conceived and so dedicated, can long endure.

In this part, Lincoln addressed the issue of the day. He equated the Civil War to a "testing" of "that nation," a nation not divided into North and South. In this test, Lincoln seemed to ask, would this creation known as the United States survive? Standing at the location where 50,000 men were killed, wounded, missing, or captured over a period of three days, Lincoln asked his audience to look away from the bloodshed to the larger issue of whether the United States could survive. While Everett's speech examined the specific events of the battle, Lincoln focused his remarks on the ideals represented by the battle, a fitting gesture for the president of the nation.

> We are met on a great battle-field of that war. We have come to dedicate a portion of that field, as a final resting place for those who here gave their lives that that nation might live. It is altogether fitting and proper that we should do this.

The Meaning of the Gettysburg Address

In three sentences in a row, Lincoln used "we" as the subject. While the use of "we" was directed to the audience before him at Gettysburg, it also applied to the nation as a whole. He was saying that "we," the nation, must review this "great battle-field" in this "great civil war." By repeating "we" and "great," Lincoln added a musical quality to his speech, and like a song or poem, it lifted his audience's attention to the task of honoring those who sacrificed their lives at Gettysburg. Their sacrifices were tied to the nation's struggle for greatness, and as president, Lincoln honored them.

> But in a larger sense, we cannot dedicate—we cannot consecrate—we cannot hallow—this ground. The brave men, living and dead, who struggled here, have consecrated it, far above our power to add or detract.

These words showed that Lincoln recognized that those at the ceremony could not make the grounds sacred, as the dead men had already done so. In many respects, Lincoln was humble and very aware that the presidency was greater than any man who bore the title.

> The world will little note, nor long remember what we say here, but it can never forget what they did here. It is for us the living, rather, to be dedicated here to the unfinished work which they who fought here have thus far so nobly advanced.

Lincoln began to move forward in time to the future, suggesting that the memories created by the event would be stronger than any words used to describe them. He then challenged his audience to be dedicated to the "unfinished work" of the men who had fought to determine that the United States, conceived under the notion that all

Executive Mansion,

Washington, _____, 186_.

Four score and seven years ago our fathers brought forth, upon this continent, a new nation, conceived in liberty, and dedicated to the proposition that "all men are created equal"

Now we are engaged in a great civil war, testing whether that nation, or any nation so conceived, and so dedicated, can long endure. We are met on a great battle field of that war. We have come to dedicate a portion of it, as a final resting place for those who died here, that the nation might live. This we may, in all propriety do. But, in a larger sense, we can not dedicate — we can not consecrate — we can not hallow, this ground — The brave men, living and dead, who struggled here, have hallowed it, far above our poor power to add or detract. The world will little note, nor long remember what we say here; while it can never forget what they did here.

It is rather for us, the living, we here be dedicat— to stand here,

---

This is the Nicolay First Draft version of Lincoln's Gettysburg Address. John Nicolay, who accompanied Lincoln to Gettysburg, claimed that this was the copy Lincoln took to the dedication ceremony. However, he recognized that it was significantly different from what Lincoln actually said.

men are created equal, would survive. The fight had to go on, Lincoln argued, and the steady repetition of the term "here" demanded of his audience that it should decide at that moment to continue the fight.

> It is rather for us to be here dedicated to the great task remaining before us—that from these honored dead we take increased devotion to that cause for which they gave the last full measure of devotion—that we here highly resolve that these dead shall not have died in vain—that this nation, under God, shall have a new birth of freedom—and that government of the people, by the people, for the people, shall not perish from the earth.

Here, Lincoln spoke of the need to pick up the cause for which the dead had given their lives, their "last full measure of devotion." He pointed in the direction of the battle, where the nation "shall have a new birth of freedom." In repeating the word "nation" five times in his speech, Lincoln underlined that the Union and Confederacy were never to be divided. Lincoln suggested that a victory by the North would result in the birth of a new nation. Its government would be "of the people, by the people, for the people." While the nation had yet to meet the ideal that all men are created equal, Lincoln painted a future ideal, a new goal, in which the government finally represented the people of the nation, all of them, whether they stood before him on that November morning in Gettysburg or read his words from a book seven score years later.

CHAPTER 5

A SPEECH THAT LIVES ON IN HISTORY

When the Battle of Gettysburg had concluded on July 3, 1863, Lincoln was elated at the outcome. He became furious, however, when General Meade failed to pursue Robert E. Lee's wounded army across the Potomac into Virginia. Meade claimed that his army was too weak and needed to bury its dead. As Lee slipped back into the South, Lincoln noted to a colleague, "Our army held the war in the hollow of their hand and they would not close it." As clearly as he envisioned a far-off future, Lincoln saw the troubles of the coming months.

The End of the War

The war carried on for another eighteen months. A year after Gettysburg, General William T. Sherman's army captured Atlanta and began its famous march to the sea. As the tide of the war turned in favor of the Union, Lincoln's popularity rose. He was re-elected in a landslide victory in November

Confederate general Robert E. Lee and Union general Ulysses S. Grant *(both seated at center, surrounded by other soldiers)* are portrayed discussing the terms of the Confederate surrender at the Appomattox Court House in 1865.

1864. In January of the following year, Congress passed the Thirteenth Amendment, which, when ratified, abolished the institution of slavery. On April 9, 1865, General Robert E. Lee surrendered the Army of Northern Virginia, the last unit of the Confederacy still fighting, on the courthouse steps in Appomattox, Virginia. The bloodiest war in American history ended, with approximately 650,000 dead.

Five days later, President Lincoln was shot dead in Ford's Theatre in Washington, D.C., by actor John Wilkes Booth. The final casualty of the war, the sixteenth president of the United States died the next day.

In this illustration, published in *Frank Leslie's Illustrated Newspaper* on May 6, 1865, John Wilkes Booth is shown escaping from President Abraham Lincoln's theater box after shooting the president on April 14. Booth was found and killed in Virginia twelve days later.

Are All Men Created Equal?

As Abraham Lincoln predicted, it would be a struggle for America to reach the ideal expressed in the Declaration of Independence and in the Gettysburg Address of equality for all men. Have we reached it yet?

In the years following the end of the war, there were attempts to heal the scars in the South, where all of the war's battles were fought except for Gettysburg. Between 1865 and 1877, federal troops were stationed in the South in an effort to protect the newly freed African Americans. Congress passed the Fourteenth and Fifteenth Amendments to the Constitution, intending to provide civil and voting rights for them. However, state governments in the South began to enact what later became known as Jim Crow laws. Named after an offensive skit performed by a white actor, these laws restricted business ownership, availability of services, voting rights, and marriage for African Americans and other nonwhites.

This Alfred R. Waud cartoon, entitled *The First Vote* and published in *Harper's Weekly* on November 16, 1867, depicts black Southern voters casting ballots for the first time.

In 1878, federal troops were pulled out of the South, several federal government bureaus closed, and the state governments were back in Southern hands. In several states, African Americans were forced to pay a special tax, called a poll tax, to vote. Few could afford to pay it.

Jim Crow laws were not restricted to the South; they were passed in states from Delaware to California. Other kinds of race-based laws

Martin Luther King Jr. is interviewed by a reporter after delivering his "I Have a Dream" speech at the Lincoln Memorial in Washington, D.C., on August 28, 1963. In demanding civil rights for African Americans, King referred to the Declaration of Independence and the Constitution as a "promissory note" that had become overdue.

were passed well into the twentieth century. As late as 1945, during World War II, Japanese American citizens along the West Coast were rounded up and taken to remote camps because of their ancestry. American women of all colors have suffered as well and were denied the right to vote until 1920.

The road that Lincoln first described at Gettysburg was indeed long. On December 1, 1955, a forty-two-year-old seamstress named Rosa Parks was arrested for refusing to give up her bus seat to a white man and move to the "colored" section at the back of the bus in Montgomery, Alabama. The civil rights movement was born.

Inspired by Martin Luther King Jr., Malcolm X, and Mahatma Gandhi, the movement struggled for equality for all through civil disobedience. Instead of fighting with guns or fists, civil rights activists, both blacks and whites, both Northerners and Southerners, let themselves be arrested, beaten, tear-gassed, and sometimes killed as their means of fighting for the ideals of which Lincoln spoke. Despite the mistreatment, these brave soldiers marched on, arm in arm, inspired by the powerful words of their leaders.

In 1963, Reverend King stood at the Lincoln Memorial where he had led the largest civil rights rally in American history. He began his speech, "Five score years ago, a great American, in whose symbolic shadow we stand signed the Emancipation Proclamation." In recalling Lincoln's acts of 100 years before, Reverend King painted a new future in his famous "I Have a Dream" speech:

> We will speed the day when all of God's children, black men and white men, Jews and Gentiles, Protestants and Catholics, will be able to join hands and sing . . . Free at last, Free at last, Thank God Almighty, I'm free at last.

In 1964, Congress passed the Twenty-fourth Amendment, which guaranteed that all citizens of age could vote. Like Lincoln before them, Martin Luther King Jr. and Malcolm X were assassinated for their commitment to the struggle for equality. They became sacrifices in the great test of the American ideal that all men are created equal.

Has America reached the end of the road to which President Lincoln pointed? Are all men, women, and children treated equally in America? Recent American events reveal continuing violence against and denial of rights to Americans based on race, color, disability, religious belief, or sexual orientation. In dozens of predominantly African American neighborhoods, there is little trust in the police to protect citizens. Across the country, gays struggle to acquire the same rights as heterosexuals. Disabled Americans continue to fight for equal access to services. While advancements have been made, equality for all in a government of the people, by the people, and for the people has yet to reach every part of the laws, governments, and minds of this nation.

There is still work to be done.

PRIMARY SOURCE TRANSCRIPTION

The Gettysburg Address

Four score and seven years ago our fathers brought forth on this continent, a new nation, conceived in Liberty, and dedicated to the proposition that all men are created equal.

Now we are engaged in a great civil war, testing whether that nation, or any nation so conceived and so dedicated, can long endure. We are met on a great battle-field of that war. We have come to dedicate a portion of that field, as a final resting place for those who here gave their lives that that nation might live. It is altogether fitting and proper that we should do this.

But in a larger sense, we cannot dedicate—we cannot consecrate—we cannot hallow—this ground. The brave men, living and dead, who struggled here, have consecrated it, far above our power to add or detract. The world will little note, nor long remember what we say here, but it can never forget what they did here. It is for us the living, rather, to be dedicated here to the unfinished work which they who fought here have thus far so nobly advanced. It is rather for us to be here dedicated to the great task remaining before us—that from these honored dead we take increased devotion to that cause for which they gave the last full measure of devotion—that we here highly resolve that these dead shall not have died in vain—that this nation, under God, shall have a new birth of freedom—and that government of the people, by the people, for the people, shall not perish from the earth.

TIMELINE

1776   July 4: The Declaration of Independence is signed, and the United States becomes a nation.

1787   November 18: The Constitution of the United States is completed, establishing a formal national government.

1789   September 25: The first ten amendments to the United States Constitution are passed by Congress.

1860   November 6: Abraham Lincoln is elected the sixteenth president of the United States.

1861   April 12: At 4:30 AM, Confederate guns fire shots at Fort Sumter in South Carolina, starting the Civil War.

1862   September 22: In a meeting with his cabinet, President Lincoln releases the preliminary Emancipation Proclamation, which frees all slaves in the Confederate states.

1863   July 1–3: The Battle of Gettysburg is fought in a small Pennsylvania town. With more than 50,000 casualties, it is the bloodiest battle of the Civil War.

1863   July 24: David Wills, a Gettysburg lawyer and businessman, writes to Pennsylvania governor

Timeline

Andrew Curtin to propose the establishment of a national cemetery for the dead at Gettysburg.

— 1863 September 23: Wills invites Edward Everett, the foremost speaker of his time, to deliver the featured speech at the ceremony dedicating the national cemetery at Gettysburg.

— 1863 November 2: President Lincoln is invited by Wills to deliver a "few appropriate remarks" at the dedication ceremony.

— 1863 November 19: Lincoln delivers the Gettysburg Address.

— 1864 November 8: Lincoln is re-elected president in a landslide.

— 1865 April 9: Confederate general Robert E. Lee surrenders his Army of Northern Virginia to Union general Ulysses S. Grant at the Appomattox Court House in Virginia. The Civil War is over.

— 1865 April 14: President Lincoln is shot by John Wilkes Booth at Ford's Theatre in Washington, D.C. He dies the next day.

— 1865 December 18: The Thirteenth Amendment is ratified, abolishing slavery in the United States.

GLOSSARY

abolition The outlawing of slavery.

casualty Someone who is killed in action, is wounded, or is missing.

civil disobedience Choosing to disobey laws in a nonviolent manner in order to create changes in law or society.

Confederate States of America The group of Southern states that left the United States after the election of Abraham Lincoln as president in 1860.

consecrate To declare or set aside as sacred.

faction A small group that splits away from a larger group over differences in belief.

hallow To make holy or to greatly respect.

moderate Having political views that appeal to the widest range of people.

orator A public speaker.

secede To separate from a nation or association.

slavery The practice of owning someone for forced labor.

Union The states of America that remained loyal to President Abraham Lincoln and his government during the Civil War.

FOR MORE INFORMATION

The Annual Gettysburg Civil War Battle Reenactment
P.O. Box 3482
Gettysburg, PA 17325-3482
(717) 338-1525
Web site: http://www.gettysburgreenactment.com

Chicago Historical Society
Clark Street at North Avenue
Chicago, IL 60614-6071
(312) 642-4600
Web site: http://www.chicagohs.org

Gettysburg Convention and Visitors Bureau
89 Steinwehr Avenue
Gettysburg, PA 17325
(717) 334-2100
Web site: http://www.gettysburg.com

The Gettysburg National Military Park
97 Taneytown Road
Gettysburg, PA 17325-2804
(717) 334-1124
Web site: http://www.nps.gov/gett

The Rosa Parks Library and Museum
251 Montgomery Street
Montgomery, AL 36104
(334) 241-8661
Web site: http://www.tsum.edu/museum

Web Sites

Due to the changing nature of Internet links, the Rosen Publishing Group, Inc., has developed an online list of Web sites related to the subject of this book. This site is updated regularly. Please use this link to access the list:

http://www.rosenlinks.com/ghds/liga

FOR FURTHER READING

Corrick, James A. *Battles of the Civil War*. San Diego, CA: Lucent Books, 1996.

Feinberg, Barbara Silberdick. *Abraham Lincoln's Gettysburg Address*. Brookfield, CT: Twenty-First Century Books, 2000.

Murphy, Jim. *The Long Road to Gettysburg*. New York: Clarion Books, 1992.

Phelan, Mary Kay. *Mr. Lincoln Speaks at Gettysburg*. New York: W. W. Norton and Company, 1966.

Richards, Kenneth G. *The Gettysburg Address* (Cornerstones of Freedom). Chicago: Children's Press, 1992.

Smith, Carter, ed. *1863: The Crucial Year* (A SourceBook on the Civil War). Brookfield, CT: The Millbook Press, 1993.

Young, Robert. *The Emancipation Proclamation: Why Lincoln Really Freed the Slaves*. New York: Dillon Press, 1994.

BIBLIOGRAPHY

Donald, David Herbert. *Lincoln*. New York: Simon & Schuster, 1995.

Feinberg, Barbara Silberdick. *Abraham Lincoln's Gettysburg Address*. Brookfield, CT: The Millbrook Press, 2000.

Library of Congress. "The Gettysburg Address." April 5, 2001. Retrieved September 22, 2003 (http://www.loc.gov/exhibits/gadd/).

Military History Online. "Battle of Gettysburg." 2000. Retrieved September 22, 2003 (http://www.militaryhistoryonline.com/gettysburg/).

Murphy, Jim. *The Long Road to Gettysburg*. New York: Clarion Books, 1992.

Phelan, Mary Kay. *Mr. Lincoln Speaks at Gettysburg*. New York: W. W. Norton and Company, 1966.

Wills, Gary. *Lincoln at Gettysburg: The Words That Remade America*. New York: Simon & Schuster, 1992.

PRIMARY SOURCE IMAGE LIST

Page 4 (top): *Lincoln at Gettysburg*, oil painting by Fletcher C. Ransom, 1938. Housed at Forest Lawn Memorial Park in Glendale, California.

Page 4 (bottom): Photograph of Confederate dead, taken by Timothy O'Sullivan on July 5, 1863. Housed at the Library of Congress Prints and Photographs Division in Washington, D.C.

Page 7: Nineteenth-century log cabin in which Lincoln was born. Photographed in 1890. Housed at the Abraham Lincoln Birthplace National Historic Site in Hodgenville, Kentucky.

Page 7 (inset): Photograph of Sarah Bush Lincoln, circa 1864. Photographer unknown. Housed at the Illinois State Historical Library in Springfield, Illinois.

Page 9: Photograph of Mary Todd Lincoln, believed to have been taken by Nicholas H. Shepherd in 1846 or 1847. Housed at the Library of Congress Prints and Photographs Division in Washington, D.C.

Page 10 (left): Photograph of Daniel Webster taken by Mathew B. Brady between 1845 and 1849. Housed at the Library of Congress Prints and Photographs Division in Washington, D.C.

Page 10 (right): Henry Clay's 1844 presidential campaign ribbon that bears his photograph.

Page 11: Whig Party campaign handbill, 1846. Housed at the Chicago Historical Society in Chicago, Illinois.

Page 12: Map of the United States, engraved by W. & A. K. Johnston in 1857. Housed at the Library of Congress Geography and Map Division in Washington, D.C.

Page 13: An Act to Organize the Territories of Nebraska and Kansas, also known as the Kansas-Nebraska Act, 1854. Housed at the National Archives in Washington, D.C.

Page 17: *Taking the Stump*, satirical Currier & Ives cartoon probably drawn by Louis Maurer, 1860. Housed at the Library of Congress Prints and Photographs Division in Washington, D.C.

Page 18: "Map of the Presidential Election of 1860," published by the Department of the Interior.

Page 19: *Bombardment of Fort Sumter*, hand-colored lithograph, published by Currier & Ives around 1861. Housed at the Library of Congress Prints and Photographs Division in Washington, D.C.

Page 20 (top): *Jefferson Davis and His Cabinet*, print, 1861. Housed at the Library of Congress Prints and Photographs Division in Washington, D.C.

Page 22: *Appearance of Cemetery Hill Previous to Pickett's Charge*, drawing by Alfred R. Waud, 1863. Housed at the Library of Congress Prints and Photographs Division in Washington, D.C.

Page 23: Photographic portrait of General George G. Meade, taken between 1860 and 1865. Housed at the Library of Congress Prints and Photographs Division in Washington, D.C.

Page 24: Photograph of dead Confederate soldiers after the Battle at Gettysburg, taken by Timothy O'Sullivan in July 1863.

Page 25: Undated photograph of David Wills.

Page 27: William Saunders's design of the Soldiers National Cemetery, 1863. Housed at the Gettysburg National Military Park in Gettysburg, Pennsylvania.

Page 29: Undated photograph of Edward Everett. Housed at the Library of Congress Prints and Photographs Division in Washington, D.C.

Page 30 (left): Photograph of John Nicolay, Abraham Lincoln, and John Hay, taken by Alexander Gardner on November 8, 1863. Housed at the Library of Congress Prints and Photographs Division in Washington, D.C.

Page 30 (right): November 2, 1863, invitation letter from David Wills to Abraham Lincoln. Housed at the Library of Congress in Washington, D.C.

Page 32: Photograph showing Lincoln's arrival at Gettysburg on November 18, 1863.

Page 35: Photograph of audience and President Lincoln at Gettysburg on November 19, 1863. Housed at the National Archives in College Park, Maryland.

Page 38: Photograph of the Soldiers National Cemetery at Gettysburg, circa 1913. Housed at the Library of Congress Prints and Photographs Division in Washington, D.C.

Page 44: The Nicolay First Draft version of the Gettysburg Address, 1863. Housed at the Library of Congress in Washington, D.C.

Page 47: Lithograph depicting the surrender of Robert E. Lee at Appomattox, circa 1867, artist unknown. Housed at the Library of Congress Prints and Photographs Division in Washington, D.C.

Page 48: Illustration depicting the escape of Lincoln's assassin, John Wilkes Booth, published in *Frank Leslie's Illustrated Newspaper* on May 6, 1865.

Page 49: *The First Vote*, cartoon by Alfred R. Waud, published in *Harper's Weekly* on November 16, 1867.

INDEX

B

Battle of Gettysburg, 5, 21–23, 25, 26, 27, 31, 39, 42, 45, 46, 49
  cemetery dedication for, 5, 27, 28, 31, 33–36, 37, 43
    soldiers wounded or killed in, 21, 22, 23, 25, 27, 31, 42, 43, 45
Beauregard, Brigadier General P. G. T., 19
Booth, John Wilkes, 47
Buford, Major General John, 21

C

civil rights, 51
Civil War, 13, 17, 19, 27, 29, 31, 39, 40, 42, 43, 47, 49
Clay, Henry, 10, 13
Confederate army, 19, 21, 22, 23, 25, 27, 47
Confederate States of America, 19, 40, 45
Constitutional Union Party, 18
Curtin, Andrew, 25, 26

D

Declaration of Independence, 16, 39, 40, 49
Democratic Party, 10, 11, 13, 15, 18, 38
Douglas, Stephen, 13, 15, 18

E

Emancipation Proclamation, 40, 51
equality, 16, 39, 42, 45, 49, 51, 52
Everett, Edward, 5, 28, 31, 33, 34, 36, 37, 42

F

Fifteenth Amendment, 49
Fourteenth Amendment, 49

G

Gandhi, Mahatma, 51
Gettysburg Address, 5, 30–31, 34, 36, 37–45, 49
Gettysburg, Pennsylvania, 5, 21, 25, 29, 30, 32, 33, 39, 43, 45

H

Hay, John, 34

I

Illinois, 5, 9, 11, 13, 15, 17, 29
  state legislature, 9, 10, 11

J

Jackson, General Stonewall, 19
Jefferson, Thomas, 40, 42
Jim Crow laws, 49

K

Kansas-Nebraska Act, 15
Kentucky, 6, 9, 18, 36
King, Martin Luther, Jr., 51, 52

L

Lee, General Robert E., 19, 21, 22, 23, 46, 47
Lincoln, Abraham
  childhood of, 6–8
  family of, 9, 11
  and Gettysburg Address, 28, 29, 30–31, 33, 34, 36, 37, 38–45, 49, 51, 52

Index

nonpolitical career of, 9
political career of, 10, 11–13, 15
and presidency, 5, 15, 17–18, 21, 26, 28, 37, 46, 47
on slavery and equality, 11–13, 39, 40, 42, 45, 49
Lincoln, Edward (son), 9
Lincoln, Mary Todd (wife), 9
Lincoln, Nancy (mother), 6
Lincoln, Robert Todd (son), 9
Lincoln, Sarah Bush (stepmother), 6–7
Lincoln, Tad (son), 9
Lincoln, Thomas (father), 6, 8
Lincoln, Willie (son), 9, 33
Logan, Stephen F., 11
Longstreet, General James, 19, 22, 23

M
Malcolm X, 51, 52
Meade, Major General George G., 21, 22, 46

N
Nicolay, John, 30, 31, 34, 36
North/Northerners, 11, 13, 18, 21, 23, 25, 28, 39, 40, 42, 45, 51

P
Pennsylvania, 21, 25, 39
Pickett, Major General George, 23
presidential election of 1860, 16, 17–19

R
Republican Party, 15, 39
Reynolds, Major General John, 21

S
Scott, General Winfield, 13
Sherman, General William T., 46
slavery/slaves, 11–12, 13, 15, 16, 17, 18, 40, 47
South/Southerners, 11, 12, 13, 15, 16, 18, 19, 21, 23, 27, 31, 38, 39, 42, 46, 49, 51

T
Taylor, General Zachary, 13
Tenth Amendment, 16, 40
Thirteenth Amendment, 47
Twenty-fourth Amendment, 51

U
Union, 16, 18, 19, 29, 31, 40, 45, 46
Union army, 21, 22, 23, 25, 27, 36
United States, 5, 13, 40, 42, 43–45
    government of, 16, 32, 49, 52
U.S. Congress, 11, 13, 15, 47, 49, 51
U.S. Constitution, 16, 18, 40, 49

W
Washington, D.C., 11, 19, 21, 36, 37, 47
Webster, Daniel, 10, 13
Whig Party, 10, 11, 13
Wills, David, 25, 26, 27, 28, 29, 30, 34

About the Author

Steven P. Olson is a freelance writer who lives in Oakland, California. Visit him at http://www.stevenolson.com.

Photo Credits

Cover (left), p. 4 (left) courtesy of Forest Lawn ® Memorial-Park Association, Glendale, CA; cover (right), pp. 4 (right), 9, 10 (left), 17, 19, 20 (top), 22, 23, 29, 30 (left), 38, 47 Library of Congress Prints and Photographs Division; pp. 7, 49 © Hulton/Archive/Getty Images; p. 10 (right) © David J. & Janice L. Frent Collection/Corbis; pp. 11, 25, 27 © Picture History 2004 LLC; p. 12 Library of Congress Geography and Map Division; pp. 13, 35 National Archives and Records Administration; pp. 14, 32, 41 © Bettmann/Corbis; p. 18 Department of the Interior; p. 20 (bottom) © Gettysburg National Military Park; p. 24, 48, 50 © Corbis; pp. 30 (right), 44 The Abraham Lincoln Papers at the Library of Congress;

Designer: Les Kanturek; **Editor:** Wayne Anderson

www.ingramcontent.com/pod-product-compliance
Lightning Source LLC
Chambersburg PA
CBHW041115070526
44584CB00002B/180